A TUNDRA Food Chain

A WHO-EATS-WHAT
Adventure in the Arctic

Rebecca Hogue Wojahn   Donald Wojahn

Lerner Publications Company
Minneapolis

For Eli and Cal. We hope this answers some of your questions.

There are many links in the chain that created this series. Thanks to Kristen McCurry Mohn, Carol Hinz, Kitty Creswell, Danielle Carnito, Sarah Olmanson, Paul Rodeen, the staff of the L. E. Phillips Memorial Library, and finally, Katherine Hogue

Lerner Publications Company
A division of Lerner Publishing Group, Inc.
241 First Avenue North
Minneapolis, MN 55401 U.S.A.

Website address: www.lernerbooks.com

Library of Congress Cataloging-in-Publication Data

Wojahn, Rebecca Hogue.
  A tundra food chain : a who-eats-what adventure in the Arctic / by Rebecca Hogue Wojahn and Donald Wojahn.
    p.   cm. — (Follow that food chain)
  Includes bibliographical references and index.
  ISBN 978-0-8225-7500-9 (lib. bdg. : alk. paper) 1. Tundra ecology—Arctic regions—Juvenile literature. 2. Food chains (Ecology)—Arctic regions—Juvenile literature. I. Wojahn, Donald. II. Title.
QH84.1.W65 2009
577.5'8616—dc22   2008027092

Manufactured in the United States of America
1 2 3 4 5 6 – BP – 14 13 12 11 10 09

Contents

Introduction
WELCOME TO THE ARCTIC TUNDRA

It's July, and the Arctic tundra is in full bloom. There's not a tree in sight, but low-growing wildflowers, sedge grasses, and shrubs carpet the ground. The ground is lumpy because of shifting from so much freezing and thawing. From above, the land looks broken up, like pieces of a jigsaw puzzle.

The summer sun shines overhead—all day and nearly all night. But despite the sunshine, there's still a chill in the air. And if you stick a shovel in the soggy, boggy ground, you will only be able to dig about 2 feet (0.6 meters) deep. Then you'll hit hard, frozen soil, called **permafrost**.

Even with these cold, harsh conditions, the tundra is full of life. Birds fly overhead, **mammals** graze on shrubs and grasses, and insects swarm everywhere. What you won't find are cold-blooded creatures like snakes, lizards, or frogs. These animals need warm temperatures to keep their body heat up. On the tundra, animals have to be able to heat themselves. That's because in just a few short months, the sunlight will fade, the marshes will freeze, the snows will blow, and the temperature will drop to 50°F (28°C) colder than the inside of your kitchen freezer. Many of the animals of the tundra will head south to a warmer climate. But other animals will stay. They have remarkable ways to survive the long, cold winter.

Arctic Ocean

EUROPE

ASIA

NORTH
AMERICA

Atlantic
Ocean

Pacific
Ocean

AFRICA

SOUTH
AMERICA

☐ tundra

The Arctic Tundra

In the Arctic tundra, the average winter temperature is −30°F (−34°C). The average summer temperature is 37 to 54°F (3 to 12°C). Because of the way Earth tilts slightly on its axis, the Arctic region is exposed to constant or nearly constant sun for a short time each summer. This is called the midnight sun. But in the winter, the Arctic region is tilted away from the sun. That causes a period of near darkness, called the polar night.

Choose a
TERTIARY CONSUMER

From the polar bear prowling over the ice to the swarms of mosquitoes, gnats, and flies buzzing over the bogs, all living things are connected in the Arctic tundra. Animals and other organisms feed on and transfer energy to one another. This relationship is called a **food chain** or a **food web**.

In food chains, the strongest **predators** are called **tertiary consumers**. They hunt other animals for food and have few natural enemies. Some of the animals they eat are **secondary consumers**. Secondary consumers are also predators. They hunt plant-eating animals. Plant eaters are **primary consumers**.

Plants are **producers**. Using energy from the sun, they produce their own food. Plants take in **nutrients** from the soil. They also provide nutrients to the animals that eat them.

Decomposers are insects or **bacteria** that break down dead plants and animals. Decomposers change them into the nutrients found in the soil.

The plants and animals in a food chain depend on one another. Sometimes there's a break in the chain, such as one type of animal dying out. This loss ripples through the rest of the **habitat**.

Begin your journey through the tundra food web by choosing a powerful **carnivore**, or meat eater. These tertiary consumers are at the top of the food chain. That means that, for the most part, they don't have any enemies in the tundra (except for humans).

When it's time for the tertiary consumer to eat, pick its meal and flip to that page. As you go through the book, don't be surprised if you backtrack and end up where you never expected to be. That's how food webs work—they're complicated. And watch out for those dead ends! When you hit one of those, you have to go back to page 7 and start over with another tertiary consumer.

The main role an animal plays in the tundra food web is identified by a color-coded shape. Here is the key to that code:

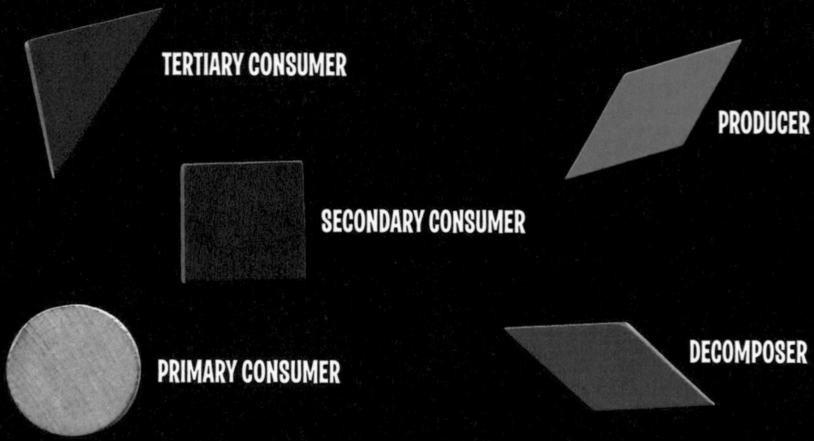

TERTIARY CONSUMER

PRODUCER

SECONDARY CONSUMER

PRIMARY CONSUMER

DECOMPOSER

To choose . . .

. . . a grizzly bear. TURN TO PAGE 8.
. . . a snowy owl. TURN TO PAGE 12.
. . . an Arctic wolf. TURN TO PAGE 30.
. . . a polar bear. TURN TO PAGE 33.
. . . a wolverine. TURN TO PAGE 37.
. . . a peregrine falcon. TURN TO PAGE 52.

To learn more about a tundra food web, GO TO PAGE 23.

GRIZZLY BEAR *(Ursus arctos horribilis)*

The young grizzly bear stretches up on his hind legs after a snack of loganberries. He may look as if he's squinting to get a better view, but what he's really doing is getting a better *smell*. He drops down to all fours lightly—despite weighing almost 1,000 pounds (454 kilograms)—and lumbers off with a purpose.

About a mile (1.6 kilometers) farther down the field, he finally sees what his nose smelled. It's a pack of wolves tearing into a musk ox calf. With a growly cough, the grizzly announces his arrival. The wolves eat faster. The bear swings his head, warning them to clear out. Then he charges at the wolves. They scatter and then dart back trying to get a few more bites of their kill. The bear charges again, this time close enough to swat one with his 4-inch (10-centimeter) claws. The wolves finally give in to his bullying and slink away.

The grizzly digs in to what's left of the musk ox. During the summer, the grizzly needs about 30 pounds (14 kg) of food a day. That's a lot of berries, so it's always nice to add some meat to his diet. Especially when it's a free meal that he didn't have to catch for himself.

Last night for dinner, the grizzly did his own hunting. He chomped down...

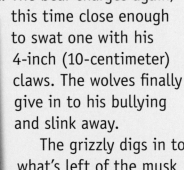

8

. . . a caribou grazing on a shrub. To see what another caribou is up to, TURN TO PAGE 20.

. . . an Arctic hare hopping across the sedges. To see what another hare is up to, TURN TO PAGE 46.

. . . an injured Arctic wolf, gored by a musk ox. To see what another wolf is up to, TURN TO PAGE 30.

. . . a musk ox calf that was sick. To see what another musk ox is up to, TURN TO PAGE 48.

. . . lots of wild blueberries. To see what the shrubs, wildflowers, and sedges of the tundra are like, TURN TO PAGE 40.

. . . a bunch of northern red-backed voles. To see what another vole is up to, TURN TO PAGE 50.

. . . a dead wolverine. To see what another wolverine is up to, TURN TO PAGE 37.

. . . a snowy owlet with an injured wing. To see what another snowy owl is up to, TURN TO PAGE 12.

ARCTIC FOX
(Alopex lagopus)

The Arctic fox hovers behind the polar bear. The dead musk ox the polar bear is feasting on smells so good! The fox trots closer. With a growl, the polar bear turns and lunges at the fox. The fox jumps back. He doesn't want to become the bear's next meal.

The fox heads back to the pile of rocks that marks his den. Inside, his cubs, his mate, and a vixen—kind of an older sister nanny for the cubs—are waiting. His ancestors have lived in this den for generations—more than two hundred years! Tunnels snake under the ground. The den has six secret exits that allow the fox family to pop up in different places outside.

He steps past a pile of goose feet—the remains of a recent family meal. His five cubs whine in disappointment when they see him come in without any dinner. If it were winter, he'd dig out some frozen, stored food. But for today, he'll have to try again later.

Or maybe not! His nose twitches. Arctic hares—and nearby! His strong sense of smell picks them up even from underground. He creeps down the tunnel. If he's lucky, his family won't be so hungry tonight.

Last night for dinner, the Arctic fox crunched . . .

Winter Wardrobe

You might not recognize the Arctic fox in December. As the days shorten and the air cools, he sheds his brown fur and grows a new white coat. This helps him to blend in with the snow. His fur actually has two layers. There's a soft, fluffy undercoat for warmth and a rougher outercoat that is waterproof. It's kind of like wearing a raincoat over a thick winter jacket. When he rests, he can wrap his tail around his body for an extra layer of warmth, just like a scarf or a blanket.

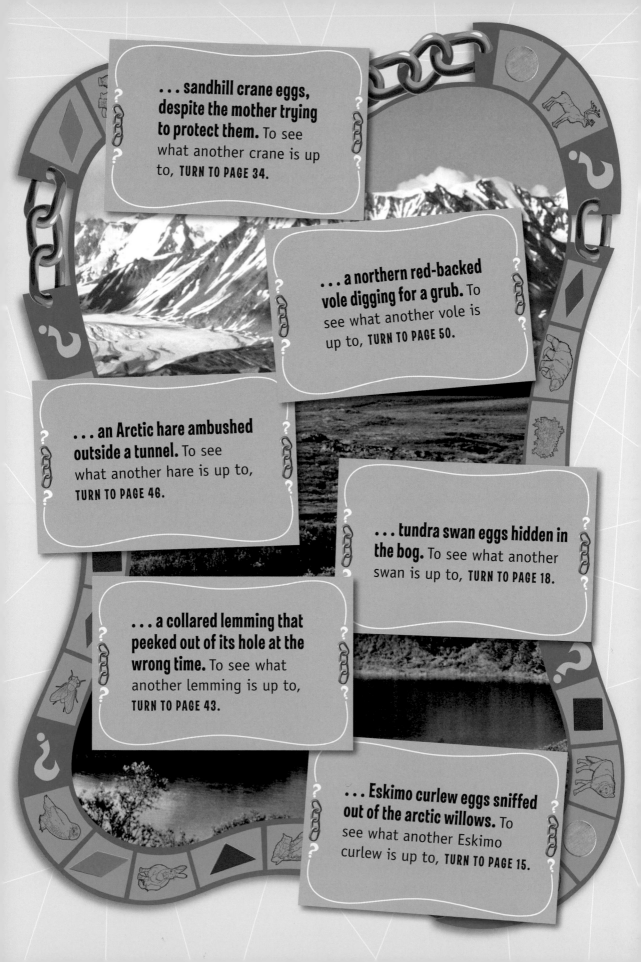

. . . sandhill crane eggs, despite the mother trying to protect them. To see what another crane is up to, TURN TO PAGE 34.

. . . a northern red-backed vole digging for a grub. To see what another vole is up to, TURN TO PAGE 50.

. . . an Arctic hare ambushed outside a tunnel. To see what another hare is up to, TURN TO PAGE 46.

. . . tundra swan eggs hidden in the bog. To see what another swan is up to, TURN TO PAGE 18.

. . . a collared lemming that peeked out of its hole at the wrong time. To see what another lemming is up to, TURN TO PAGE 43.

. . . Eskimo curlew eggs sniffed out of the arctic willows. To see what another Eskimo curlew is up to, TURN TO PAGE 15.

SNOWY OWL *(Nyctea scandiaca)*

A shadow sweeps over the field of Arctic willows. It's the only warning that a snowy owl is hunting here. Other kinds of birds make flapping sounds when they fly. But the snowy owl's flight is nearly silent. Soft edges on his wing feathers reduce the noise and allow him to sneak up on **prey**. This is important because snowy owls don't hunt under the cover of night as other owls do. Snowy owls hunt in the full light of day. With the sun shining almost twenty-hour hours a day in the summer, they have to. If they waited for darkness, they'd starve.

This snowy owl swoops down, stretches out his sharp talons, and snags a lemming off the ground. But it's not for him. He flies back to the female he's courting and adds the fresh kill to the pile he's building. She studies the offering with her yellow eyes. She blinks. Then she takes off. It's a good sign. The male snowy owl grabs the lemming and follows her. High up in the air, he hands it to

360° Vision

The snowy owls' large yellow eyes help them see well for hunting. In fact, their eyes are so large that they can't move in their eye sockets like ours do. Instead, snowy owls must move their entire head to look left or right. This is true of all owls. But it's not true that owls can turn their heads all the way around. They can twist them to look behind them, but then they must face front again before turning the other way.

A female *(left)* and male snowy owl

her. When she takes it, they circle back down, looking for a place to build their nest. They settle on a spot on the ground. Since trees don't grow in the tundra, she'll scratch out a nest in a mound of dirt. They are ready to start their family.

   Last night for dinner, the snowy owl ate...

A snowy owl brings a mouse to its chicks.

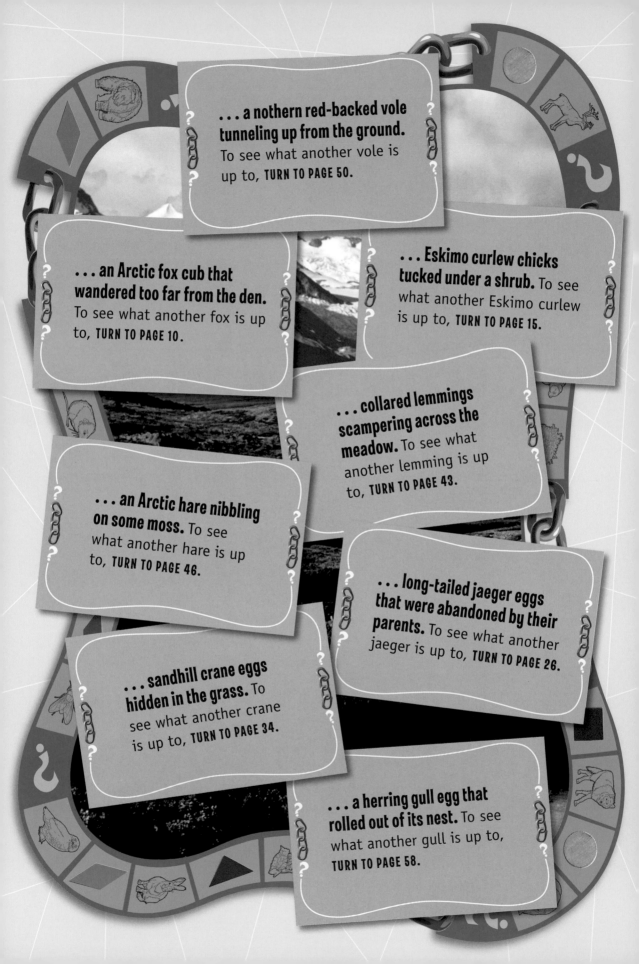

... a nothern red-backed vole tunneling up from the ground. To see what another vole is up to, TURN TO PAGE 50.

... an Arctic fox cub that wandered too far from the den. To see what another fox is up to, TURN TO PAGE 10.

... Eskimo curlew chicks tucked under a shrub. To see what another Eskimo curlew is up to, TURN TO PAGE 15.

... collared lemmings scampering across the meadow. To see what another lemming is up to, TURN TO PAGE 43.

... an Arctic hare nibbling on some moss. To see what another hare is up to, TURN TO PAGE 46.

... long-tailed jaeger eggs that were abandoned by their parents. To see what another jaeger is up to, TURN TO PAGE 26.

... sandhill crane eggs hidden in the grass. To see what another crane is up to, TURN TO PAGE 34.

... a herring gull egg that rolled out of its nest. To see what another gull is up to, TURN TO PAGE 58.

ESKIMO CURLEW (*Numenius borealis*)

DEAD END. While Eskimo curlews haven't been declared **extinct**, they are critically **endangered**. No one has officially spotted one in almost forty years This speckled, curve-billed bird once clouded the skies in huge flocks as it **migrated** from the tundra to South America. But the birds were also tasty to eat. In the 1800s, they were hunted nearly out of existence. In 1916 a law was passed to protect Eskimo curlews. But by then, one of their favorite foods, the Rocky Mountain locust, had gone extinct. Without its favorite food, the curlew population continued to shrink. Many people hold out hope that the Eskimo curlew still flies somewhere on the tundra.

This is a drawing of an Eskimo curlew.

AMPHIPOD *(Amphipoda)*

The amphipod scoots on seven pairs of legs through the loose, wet leaves. His shrimplike body is only a half-inch (1.3 centimeters) long. He's on a mission to find a mate. He won't go too far, though. This spot near the marsh's edge has the perfect amount of moisture. Without a hard shell, his body soaks up the water around him. Too much or too little and he'll die.

A red-throated loon comes ashore, also searching for a partner. As the loon waddles by, he stirs up the amphipod's patch of dirt. Exposed, the amphipod uses his tail to flip himself quickly out of the bird's way.

He squeezes under a stone and finds a swarm of fellow amphipods, bumping around in the loose soil. (Sometimes they're called beach fleas because they look like fleas jumping around on an animal.) Here he'll find his mate and start his family.

Of course, that really doesn't mean much to him. He won't stick around to care for the little amphipods. He'll already be off, munching away on the dead plants and animals of the tundra, helping them to decompose as he goes.

Last night for dinner, he dined on . . .

Amphipods Everywhere

Maybe you have never heard of an amphipod before. But if you've ever turned over a rock, chances are you've seen them. Different kinds of amphipods are found all over the world. They live on land and in lakes and oceans. In fact, they like moisture so much that they sometimes cause problems for swimming pool owners. Amphipods get in the water and clog the filters.

. . . **bacteria that are slowly breaking down a dead tundra swan.** To see what another swan is up to, TURN TO PAGE 18.

. . . **dead leaves from Arctic willows.** To see what the shrubs, wildflowers, and sedges of the tundra are like, TURN TO PAGE 40.

TUNDRA SWAN *(Cygnus columbianus)*

The tundra swan dad, or cob, arranges himself on his nest of eggs. As he plumps up his feathers, many fall out and float off in the light breeze. He's nearly as helpless as the eggs he's tending while he **molts**, or loses his old feathers and grows new ones. He even loses the feathers he uses to fly, so he can't fly away from predators until his new ones grow in.

Nearby, his mate, called a pen, paddles around in the water. She dips her long neck underwater and yanks at the plants. She pulls her head up fast at the sudden honking and hissing from the cob. It's a wolverine, prowling near the nest!

She launches herself toward the wolverine, flapping her wings. Her wings are as long as he is. Their hard edges smack him across the face repeatedly. Meanwhile, the cob nips and pecks from behind. The wolverine is overpowered and gives up, looking for something easier to eat.

The pair doesn't have much time to settle. With a honk, the cob warns about a grizzly bear approaching in the distance. The bear hasn't seen them yet, but the swans know he's too big to fight. So instead, they both take to the water. Maybe they can draw the bear away from the nest and protect their eggs that way. It's risky, but it's their only chance. They nervously nibble on water bugs and wait to see if the bear will come their way.

Last night for dinner, the pair of swans gulped down . . .

These swans are sitting on their nest.

18

. . . an Arctic springtail or two drifting in the cold water. To see what another springtail is up to, TURN TO PAGE 28.

. . . leaves and stems from some wildflowers. To see what the shrubs, wildflowers, and sedges of the tundra are like, TURN TO PAGE 40.

. . . bits of lichen and moss. To see what the lichens and mosses of the tundra are like, TURN TO PAGE 24.

. . . a woolly bear caterpillar just thawing out. To see what another caterpillar is up to, TURN TO PAGE 38.

. . . a pesky horsefly circling overhead. To see what other horseflies, mosquitoes, and gnats are up to, TURN TO PAGE 56.

. . . amphipods under a stone. To see what another amphipod is up to, TURN TO PAGE 16.

CARIBOU *(Rangifer tarandus)*

Zzzzzzt! The white-maned old caribou twitches his ears, jiggles his head, and ripples his back. Still the flies and mosquitoes buzz around him. He runs for a short distance. The wind he creates by running helps shoo the bugs off him. But he returns to the safety of the herd, and it's not long until the insects have found him again. He pants. He's almost worn out—just from fighting the flies!

As strange as it may seem, mosquitoes, horseflies, and gnats are serious predators of caribou. Each week of summer, a caribou may lose a half-gallon (2 liters) of blood from bug bites. That makes him lose weight and get weak, so he does everything he can to get rid of them. But the flying insects cause more problems than just itchy bites. Earlier, flies laid eggs on his leg hair. The eggs have hatched, and the **larvae** are crawling up to his back. They'll burrow under his skin to finish growing, feeding off him and leaving his hide bubbly and lumpy.

The caribou shakes again. Maybe if he goes into the lake he'll get some relief. But wait! Suddenly, the herd is alert. Another male rears up. Then, head up, tail up, and ears forward, he extends one leg out to the side. That means danger!

The rest of the herd spy the danger—wolves. They gather together and rush off noisily—their legs click, their antlers clack, and their fawns cry. But the herd is moving too fast for the old caribou. He finds himself separated from his group—and the wolves circle closer. He rears up with his hooves and kicks at the growling pack. They back up and then come at him again. This time, he lowers his antlers and sweeps them across the snarling crowd. He snags a wolf in its side. With a whimper, the wolf limps away. The rest of the pack follows his retreat.

The caribou makes his way up a small hill where his herd has regrouped. There's still snow in patches up here. Breathing heavily, the caribou paws at the ground with his oversized hoof. Because of the snow on the ground, there's less to eat here, but there are also fewer mosquitoes. He turns up some roots, yanks them out with his lip, and grinds them against the top of his mouth. He needs to build up his strength again.

Last night for dinner, the caribou ground up...

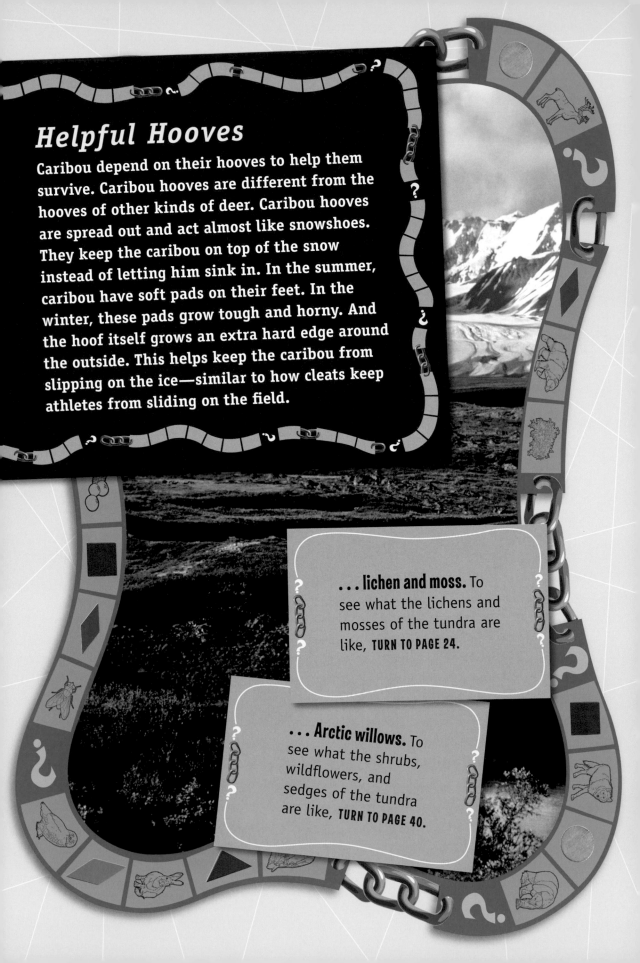

Helpful Hooves

Caribou depend on their hooves to help them survive. Caribou hooves are different from the hooves of other kinds of deer. Caribou hooves are spread out and act almost like snowshoes. They keep the caribou on top of the snow instead of letting him sink in. In the summer, caribou have soft pads on their feet. In the winter, these pads grow tough and horny. And the hoof itself grows an extra hard edge around the outside. This helps keep the caribou from slipping on the ice—similar to how cleats keep athletes from sliding on the field.

. . . lichen and moss. To see what the lichens and mosses of the tundra are like, **TURN TO PAGE 24.**

. . . Arctic willows. To see what the shrubs, wildflowers, and sedges of the tundra are like, **TURN TO PAGE 40.**

A TUNDRA FOOD WEB

Energy moves around the food chain from the sun to plants, from plants to plant eaters, and from animals to the creatures that eat them. Energy also moves from dead animals to the plants and animals that draw nutrients from them.

LICHENS AND MOSSES

Plants need three things to survive—water, sunlight, and nutrients from the soil. In the tundra, it is often dry and dark and the dirt is frozen solid. You'd think the land would be bare, but the plants still manage to grow. In the few weeks of summer, the land becomes a multicolored carpet. Velvety greens, like sphagnum moss, spread over the ground. They take in moisture from the air. These plants don't need roots running deep in the ground. Instead, they send out tiny rootlets across the ground and shoot up small sprouts.

Even the rocks have color. Crusty lichens cover the stones and provide additional food for the tundra animals. Lichens are actually two plants that grow together—fungus that sticks to the rock and algae that grows on top of it, soaking up the summer sunlight and giving it color. Some of the lichens can grow for centuries. Greenland lichen can be 4,500 years old!

Because moss and lichen are such simple plants, they are very sensitive to pollution. Scientists have studied them for more than thirty years to watch how air quality has changed in the tundra.

So far, these tundra producers are doing okay. *Last night for dinner, they soaked up nutrients from . . .*

Above: A close-up of lichen
Below: Rocks covered with lichens, mosses, and other small plants

. . . polar bear dung.
To see what another
polar bear is up to,
TURN TO PAGE 33.

**. . . amphipods eating
the dead matter.** To
see what another
amphipod is up to,
TURN TO PAGE 16.

**. . . tunnels made by the
collared lemmings.** Lemmings
help to stir up the soil. To
see what another lemming
is up to, TURN TO PAGE 43.

**. . . Arctic springtails in
the mud.** To see what
another springtail is
up to, TURN TO PAGE 28.

LONG-TAILED JAEGER *(Stercorarius longicaudus)*

The long-tailed jaeger wings in from the sea for his summer vacation in the Arctic. He soars gracefully over the blooming tundra. He's just completed a 7,000-mile (11,265-kilometer) flight from the southeast coast of South America. That's like traveling from the eastern coast to the western coast of the United States—three times! And in August, he'll head south again as the cold comes back over the tundra. He'll spend most of his winter out over the sea, far from land.

The jaeger perches on a mound of grass. Nearby, a herring gull fluffs her feathers and gives a warning cry. She must have a nest somewhere close. The jaeger flies off, snapping at flying insects as he goes. He spots a falcon with a lemming clenched in her talons. He makes a swoop at her catch. They tug in midair for a moment, and then the falcon breaks free with the lemming tight in her grip.

The jaeger circles around. He hasn't forgotten the gull. And now the gull has gone off hunting. The jaeger soon uncovers her nest in the dirt. Gulp. He swallows an egg. Then the gull's mate comes flapping and screeching at him. And the jaeger is off again.

Last night for dinner, the jaeger swallowed . . .

A long-tailed jaeger eats a collared lemming.

26

Jaeger GPS

So how do birds like jaegers know where to go when flying around the globe? Scientists know that birds use landmarks on the ground as well as the patterns of the stars and the sun to find their way. They also have a mineral called magnetite in their heads. This helps them keep track of Earth's magnetic fields and may help them sense direction. We still have a lot to learn about seabirds like the jaeger.

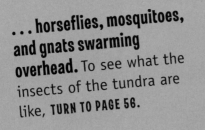

. . . horseflies, mosquitoes, and gnats swarming overhead. To see what the insects of the tundra are like, **TURN TO PAGE 56.**

. . . collared lemmings on the move to a new home. To see what another lemming is up to, **TURN TO PAGE 43.**

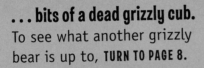

. . . bits of a dead grizzly cub. To see what another grizzly bear is up to, **TURN TO PAGE 8.**

. . . Eskimo curlew eggs just laid yesterday. To see what another Eskimo curlew is up to, **TURN TO PAGE 15.**

. . . sandhill crane eggs just starting to hatch. To see what another crane is up to, **TURN TO PAGE 34.**

. . . a tundra swan egg neglected by a parent for a minute. To see what another swan is up to, **TURN TO PAGE 18.**

. . . a northern red-backed vole scratching out a new tunnel. To see what another vole is up to, **TURN TO PAGE 50.**

. . . a herring gull chick waiting for a meal. To see what another gull is up to, **TURN TO PAGE 58.**

ARCTIC SPRINGTAIL *(Onychiurus arcticus)*

The springtail rests on top of the puddle. In fact, the whole puddle is coated with the newly hatched insects. His mouthparts suck in tiny bits of algae and rotten plants—a decomposer's delight—that float on the surface. As he drifts toward the edge of the puddle, a running lemming splashes him up onto land. The lemming scratches the dirt, and the springtail hops out of the way. He doesn't have any wings for flying, but underneath his front side is a special arm called a furcula. When he needs to escape, he flicks it down against the ground. This springs him 4 to 5 inches (10 to 13 centimeters) away—usually far enough to get him to safety.

Most insects that live through the tundra winter have a substance that allows them to survive being frozen. The springtail is different. His body supercools in winter. That means the temperature at which his body will freeze lowers, so he's able to live through colder temperatures in winter than he could in summer. This process also sheds water from his body. This drier body and colder freezing point allow him to remain unfrozen through the winter.

Last night for dinner, he sipped...

Arctic springtails are so small, this photo had to be taken with an electron microscope.

Hopping All Over the World

Springtails don't just live in the tundra—they're all over the planet. They "spring up" wherever there is moisture. Sometimes people think they bite, but their mouths really aren't able to bite humans. What feels like a bite is probably the little prick that the furcula makes when it snaps against a person's skin as the springtail hops away.

. . . **bits of mold from the decaying tundra plants and shrubs.** To see what the shrubs, wildflowers, and sedges of the tundra are like, TURN TO PAGE 40.

. . . **bits of algae and fungus from the lichen and moss.** To see what the mosses and lichens of the tundra are like, TURN TO PAGE 24.

ARCTIC WOLF *(Canis lupus arctos)*

The female wolf jogs along with her pack. The musk ox herd has noticed them and is gathering together. The wolves circle around the herd, golden eyes gleaming and white fur glowing in the sun. They keep moving, pulling in closer, until the musk oxen panic and bolt.

A wolf pack takes down a musk ox.

30

Then the alpha male, the pack's leader, makes his move. With flashing teeth, he strikes the neck of an older musk ox who has fallen behind. Instantly, the female wolf jumps at the musk ox too, followed by the rest of the pack. The other musk oxen dash away to safety. In slow motion, the pack's combined weight brings the musk ox down. The alpha male makes sure the musk ox is dead and then starts feasting. The female wolf stands back, panting and waiting for her turn. As the alpha male's mate, she'll eat next. Then the younger wolves will take their turn.

"White Wolves"

Arctic wolves are related to gray wolves. They are similar, but they have a few differences—mostly ones that help them survive the cold and dark. Arctic wolves have white coats instead of gray, which help them blend in to the snowy background. They also have short ears, legs, and muzzles, which hold in body heat better than longer body parts do. Finally, their eyes are different. They've got a special layer of cells that helps them to see during the months when it is dark all day and all night.

When the wolves have eaten their fill, they leave the remains for the gulls and wolverines. The wolves make the long 12-mile (19-kilometer) trek back to their den. Waiting in the rock cave are two pups—the first the female wolf has had in two years. They lick her, and she wags her tail. A moment or two later, the alpha male spits up some of his meal and the pups trip over themselves to gobble down the warm musk ox meat.

The wolves hunt every night, but they aren't usually so successful. *Last night for dinner, they caught . . .*

. . . **a caribou fawn tucked under a shrub.** To see what another caribou is up to, TURN TO PAGE 20.

. . . **collared lemmings.** Lots of lemmings. To see what another lemming is up to, TURN TO PAGE 43.

. . . **another musk ox weak from the winter.** To see what another musk ox is up to, TURN TO PAGE 48.

. . . **a northern red-backed vole just starting a new tunnel.** To see what another vole is up to, TURN TO PAGE 50.

. . . **an Arctic hare that just wasn't fast enough.** To see what another hare is up to, TURN TO PAGE 46.

POLAR BEAR *(Ursus maritimus)*

The polar bear stalks through the sedge grasses. Now that it's summer, the ice where she normally hunts is melting, so she's forced to do more hunting inland. In fact, finding food is getting harder and harder for her. The ice and snow that she depends on for hunting seals and whales melts sooner each year because of warmer temperatures in the tundra. Like most polar bears, she's grown thinner and has had fewer cubs in recent years. While not officially **endangered** yet, many people are very worried about the polar bear's future. That's why this is a *DEAD END.*

Wash up after Dinner

Polar bears love to punch holes in the ice and wait for seals to pop up their heads. Once the prey is killed, polar bears will eat only the fat, or blubber, of their catch, tearing it off with their forty-two sharp teeth. When they're done eating, they roll on the snow to clean up. Having blood and grease on their fur makes them cold.

33

Not only is their ice melting, but polar bears also are in danger because of high levels of toxins, or poisons, in their bodies. Pollution from around the planet ends up in the Arctic. Animals lower in the food chain eat the poisoned food. Since polar bears are tertiary consumers at the top of the chain, they eat lots of the smaller animals—and all the toxins from them build up in the polar bears' bodies. No one is sure what the results of this poisoning will be for future generations of polar bears.

SANDHILL CRANE *(Grus canadensis)*

The sandhill crane arrives at her summer spot on the wet bogs of the Arctic tundra after flapping for hundreds of miles. She's spent every summer of her life here so far. She sinks her long, skinny legs into the cool water and wades as she scoops up bugs and plants and swallows them down.

Across from her, a male crane is doing the same. He slowly bobs his way to her across the shallow water. Soon he is bowing to her and flapping his huge wings—they are nearly as wide across as the length of your bed! She ignores him at first, but soon she joins in. They dance and sing, stepping backward and forward, leaping into the air, and trumpeting calls that echo for miles. When they've decided they make a good pair, they mate and then start looking for the perfect place to make a home.

They find a spot near the bog, hidden behind some shrubs. There they gather stems and moss to line their nest. Soon, the female will lay an egg. A second one follows in a day or two. The cranes are good parents, taking turns warming the eggs and fighting off anything that comes too near. They successfully hatch both crane chicks.

Two sandhill cranes guard their chicks.

A flock of sandhill cranes takes off.

But the crane parents don't realize that a fox has come to visit. They are leading their newborn chicks to the water to let them explore. While they poke and jab at the soggy ground, the fox steals up behind them. Too late, the parents notice him and try to shoo him off. The mother even hobbles around, acting like her wing is broken—anything to draw the fox away from her chicks, who can't yet fly.

But the fox is hungry. He doesn't leave until one of the crane chicks is clamped in his jaws. It's a loss to the crane family, but one of the crane chicks wouldn't have survived anyway. Even if a predator hadn't gotten him, his brother might have. Usually, one crane chick is bossier than the other. The bossy chick hogs the food, and the other chick goes hungry and soon dies.

Last night for dinner, the cranes scarfed down...

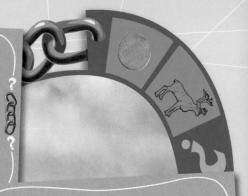

. . . **a woolly bear caterpillar rolled in a ball.** To see what another caterpillar is up to, **TURN TO PAGE 38.**

. . . **a hundred Arctic springtails.** To see what another springtail is up to, **TURN TO PAGE 28.**

. . . **stems from tundra plants.** To see what the shrubs, wildflowers, and sedges of the tundra are like, **TURN TO PAGE 40.**

. . . **moss from a stone.** To see what the lichens and mosses of the tundra are like, **TURN TO PAGE 24.**

. . . **gnats and fly larvae in the water.** To see what other horseflies, mosquitoes, and gnats are up to, **TURN TO PAGE 56.**

. . . **a northern red-backed vole, swallowed whole.** To see what another vole is up to, **TURN TO PAGE 50.**

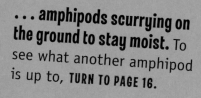

. . . **amphipods scurrying on the ground to stay moist.** To see what another amphipod is up to, **TURN TO PAGE 16.**

. . . **a baby collared lemming.** To see what another lemming is up to, **TURN TO PAGE 43.**

WOLVERINE *(Gulo gulo)*

37

The beady-eyed wolverine scratches at the dirt with her five long claws. Over the winter, she hid part of an Arctic hare here, but it's too warm now. It was stolen long ago when the ground started to thaw. Luckily, she soon comes across a dead caribou fawn, abandoned by its mother. With her extra-strong teeth and jaws, she crunches right through the fawn's bones.

Despite being willing to eat a wide variety of foods—from **carrion** to cranberries—wolverines are in danger in the wild. Their population is shrinking every year. People are working to have the U.S. Fish and Wildlife Service add wolverines to the **endangered** species list. Until wolverines are protected, this is a *DEAD END*.

WOOLLY BEAR CATERPILLAR
(Gynaephora groenlandica)

With a tiny wiggle, the woolly bear caterpillar inches across the lichen-covered rock. He rests, bathing in the sun for a few moments. Then he creeps off the stone in search of a snack. He's out of luck—he's in a bunch of Arctic willow, and Arctic willow is poisonous to him. He continues onward. A shadow passes overhead, but whatever predator it is, it doesn't spot the caterpillar. He's survived twelve summers like this so far. That's right—this caterpillar is probably older than you are! He can grow only in the summer, and because the summer is so short—just six to ten weeks—it takes him a long time to become an adult. In two more years, he will make a cocoon. Then finally he will become an Isabella tiger moth.

Last night for dinner, the woolly bear caterpillar nibbled on . . .

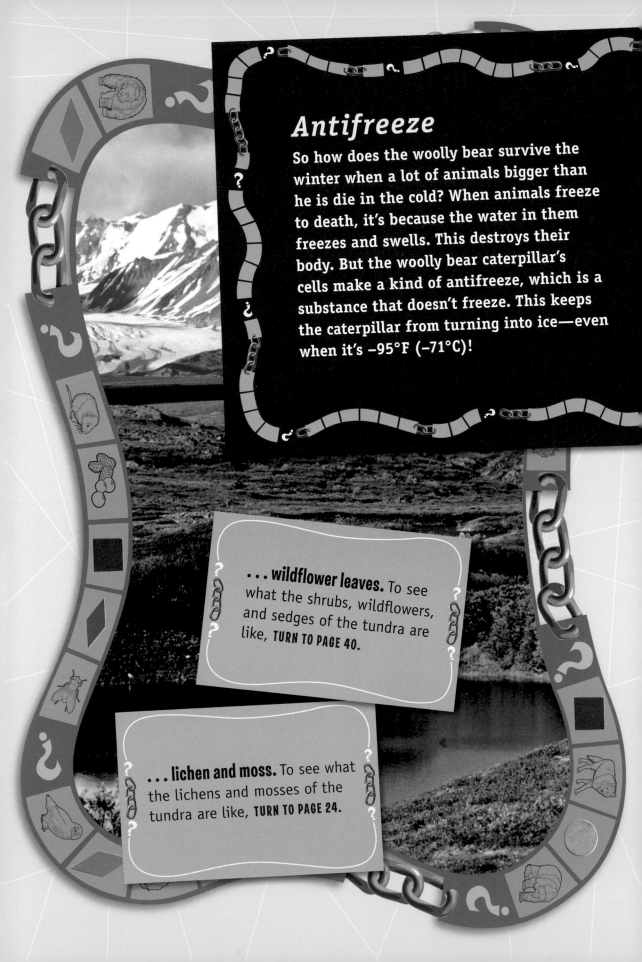

Antifreeze

So how does the woolly bear survive the winter when a lot of animals bigger than he is die in the cold? When animals freeze to death, it's because the water in them freezes and swells. This destroys their body. But the woolly bear caterpillar's cells make a kind of antifreeze, which is a substance that doesn't freeze. This keeps the caterpillar from turning into ice—even when it's −95°F (−71°C)!

... **wildflower leaves.** To see what the shrubs, wildflowers, and sedges of the tundra are like, **TURN TO PAGE 40.**

... **lichen and moss.** To see what the lichens and mosses of the tundra are like, **TURN TO PAGE 24.**

SHRUBS, WILDFLOWERS, AND SEDGES

You might recognize some of the flowers and plants of the tundra by name, but probably not by sight. Artic willows are related to willow trees, but Arctic willows are much shorter. They grow no higher than your sneakers. Yellow poppies, lavender lousewort, blueberries, thimbleberries, and cranberries hug the ground. The icy permafrost doesn't allow their roots to grow deep enough for these plants to gain any height. **Tussocks**—rounded hills of sedge grasses such as kobresia—give the ground a lumpy, bumpy look.

Because the growing season is so short—sometimes only six weeks before it starts freezing again—most of the producers of the tundra are **perennial**. That means that instead of growing from seeds in the spring, the plants store food in their leaves and stems and regrow each year. Their leaves are small, thick, hairy, and dark green, which helps them take in as much moisture as possible from the dry air.

Tussocks covered with snow during the Arctic winter

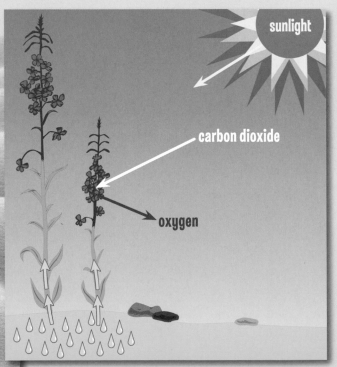

sunlight

carbon dioxide

oxygen

Plants make food and oxygen through photosynthesis. Plants draw in carbon dioxide (a gas found in air) and water. Then they use the energy from sunlight to turn the carbon dioxide and water into their food.

Many flowers are **heliotropic**, meaning they face toward the sun. As the sun changes positions in the sky, the bowl-shaped heliotropic flowers turn to follow it, soaking up as much light and warmth as they can.

The tundra's soil doesn't offer much nutrition. The cold and ice slow the decay of plants and animals, so their nutrients aren't easily released. But tundra plants soak up whatever nutrients they find.

Last night for dinner, they survived on nutrients left behind by...

Top: A dwarf willow
Bottom: The tundra is covered with dwarf birch, willows, lichens, blueberry plants, and tundra grass.

41

. . . a grizzly bear, gobbling up berries. Later on, when he poops, his dung is full of seeds. He's just helped the berries to plant themselves in a new location. To see what another grizzly is up to, TURN TO PAGE 8.

. . . wolverine dung. To see what a wolverine is up to, TURN TO PAGE 37.

. . . tunnels made by northern red-backed voles. They help to stir up the soil. To see what another vole is up to, TURN TO PAGE 50.

. . . amphipods eating the dead matter. To see what another amphipod is up to, TURN TO PAGE 16.

. . . caribou dung. To see what a caribou is up to, TURN TO PAGE 20.

. . . Arctic springtails hopping through the dirt. To see what another springtail is up to, TURN TO PAGE 28.

COLLARED LEMMINGS *(Dicrostonyx groenlandicus)*

The roof of the lemmings' tunnel crashes down on them as the heavy snow begins to melt. They have lived in this shallow maze all winter, staying warm and raising their families. They fed themselves on roots and dead grasses, which they scraped out of the dirt using extra powerful winter claws called shields. But their shields have fallen off now that summer has come, and it's time to come to the surface.

A mother lemming scratches her way out of the maze, her recent litter of babies following her. They leave behind a nest and tunnels lined with her white winter fur. She and the hundreds of other lemmings around her sport their brown summer coats now.

43

Population Explosion

About every four years, there are so many lemmings that they must leave home to find more food. These same years, there are also more Arctic foxes and more snowy owls. That's because foxes and owls feed on lemmings, and when their food supply is plentiful, they have more babies too. But with so many lemmings eating plants, they soon pick the tundra bare. So the lemmings move on. Many don't make it, and the number of lemmings drops. When that happens, many foxes and owls starve too. Then slowly, year after year, the lemming population grows again—until there are too many and it starts all over again.

A collared lemming has thicker, whiter fur during the winter.

She scurries over the ground, looking for something fresh to gnaw on. But everywhere she looks, there are lemmings—too many to be fed by the plants of the tundra here. With so many hungry lemmings attacking the plants, there soon won't be anything left to eat. Already a crowd of lemmings is moving off, looking for a new place to live. The mother lemming squeaks at her babies, letting them know to follow the group. The young lemmings were born just a few weeks ago, but already they're almost adults. They hardly listen. They'll decide for themselves whether to go or stay.

The mother lemming starts to run and joins the group. Good thing she ate last night. The group scampers over the **tussocks** of grass and across the chopped-up ground of the tundra. The lemming sees a lake—a large puddle, really—ahead. The water will be cold, but the rest of the group doesn't hesitate, and neither does she. She leaps into the freezing water. She paddles as hard as she can. Next to her, a swooping falcon snags a lemming. On her other side, cold and confused lemmings are drowning. Somehow, she manages to crawl up the other shore and continue the journey.

This lemming takes a break and nibbles at pink fireweed. *Last night for dinner, she gnawed at . . .*

. . . **more wildflowers and grasses.** To see what the shrubs, wildflowers, and sedges of the tundra are like, TURN TO PAGE 40.

. . . **lichen and moss on the side of a rock.** To see what the lichens and mosses of the tundra are like, TURN TO PAGE 24.

ARCTIC HARE *(Lepus arcticus)*

The Arctic hare nibbles at the lavender lousewort leaves. He's only a few weeks old, but already he's on his own. An Arctic fox comes sniffing by. The hare freezes. He's known this trick since he was just days old. With his summer coat of grayish brown, he looks just like a stone. The fox trots on, but then he returns, sniffing again. The hare bolts, stretching out his long feet and covering the length of your classroom in about two bounds. The fox chases but then spies something easier. From a safe distance, the hare watches as one of his neighbor hares becomes the fox's next meal.

As the weather turns colder in fall, the hare's coat will turn too. In winter, he's white, with black tips on his ears. He isn't just a white rabbit with supersized hind feet. He's perfectly adapted to the tundra's cold climate. Like most tundra animals, he has two coats—a fluffy undercoat that keeps in the warmth and a longer, silkier coat of guard hairs that helps him stay dry. And in the winter, all those hare neighbors will help him in a different way. They'll huddle together to keep warm.

But winter is a long time off—a few weeks anyway. For now it's time to eat.

Last night for dinner, the Arctic hare munched on...

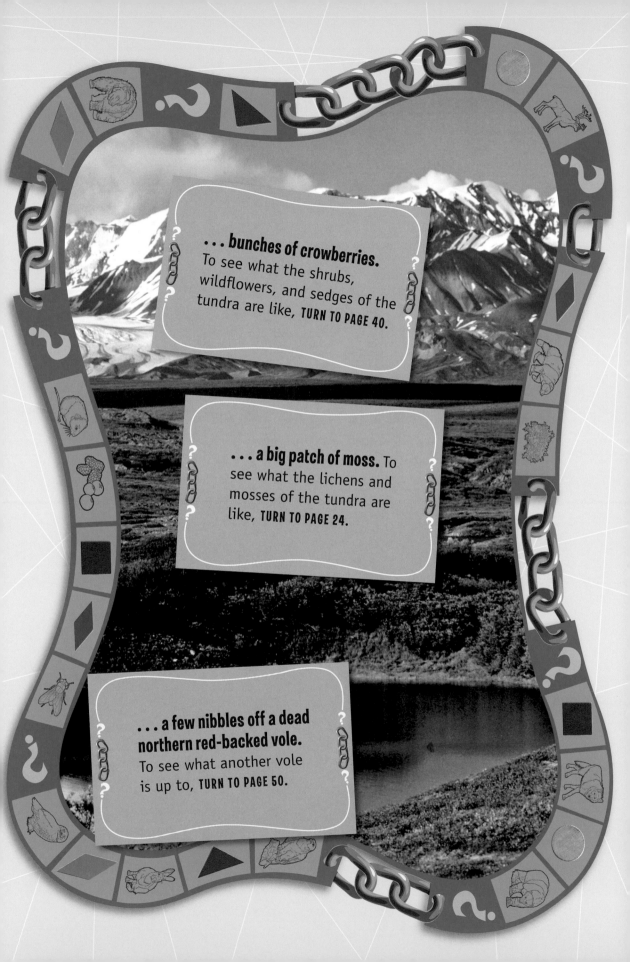

. . . bunches of crowberries. To see what the shrubs, wildflowers, and sedges of the tundra are like, TURN TO PAGE 40.

. . . a big patch of moss. To see what the lichens and mosses of the tundra are like, TURN TO PAGE 24.

. . . a few nibbles off a dead northern red-backed vole. To see what another vole is up to, TURN TO PAGE 50.

MUSK OX *(Ovibos moschatus)*

The old musk ox chomps on his cud—old grass he's spit up to chew again. Out of the corner of his eye, he sees the pesky newcomer. This new bull has been moving closer all morning. The older musk ox lowers his head and shakes his curved horns in warning. This is his territory.

Suddenly, the young challenger squares off 50 feet (15 m) from him. Then he charges. The older bull lowers his head—and his deadly horns. The two come together in a terrific crack. The older bull shoves as hard as he can, trying to throw the younger one off balance. If he can just get at the other bull's side, he can hook him with a horn, and that'll be the end of it. But the younger one is strong. And he's trying his best to do the same to the older male.

Just then a female stamps and snorts. Wolves! The males' standoff is interrupted. The herd gathers together as the wolves circle. The calves are pushed to the center, while the adult oxen stand shoulder to shoulder. The adults lower their heads and point their dangerous horns at the predators. The wolves decide it's not worth the risk. They just aren't hungry enough. They slink off to find easier **prey**.

Slowly, the musk oxen relax and start grazing again. *Last night for dinner, they chewed on . . .*

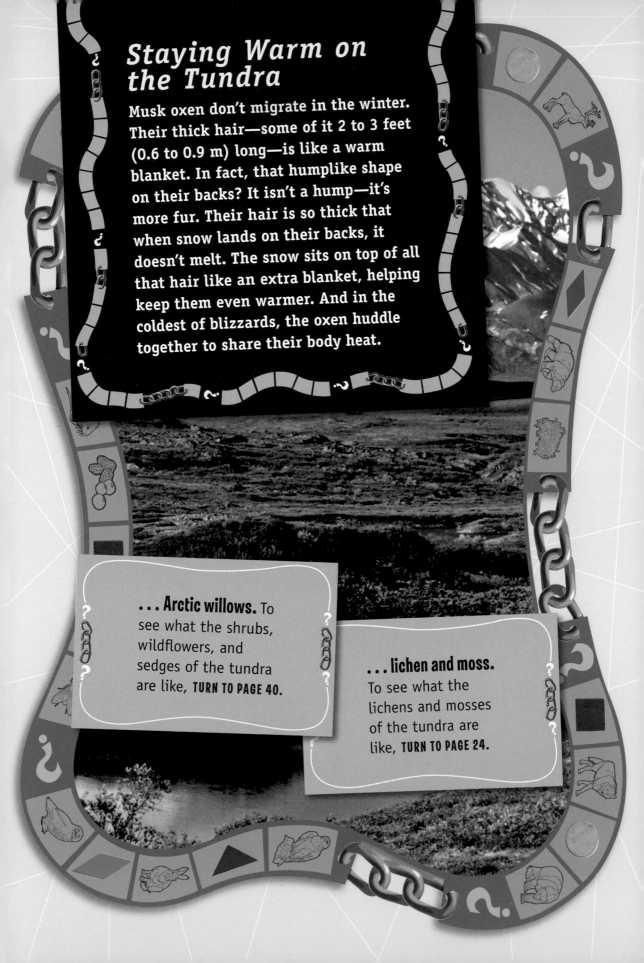

Staying Warm on the Tundra

Musk oxen don't migrate in the winter. Their thick hair—some of it 2 to 3 feet (0.6 to 0.9 m) long—is like a warm blanket. In fact, that humplike shape on their backs? It isn't a hump—it's more fur. Their hair is so thick that when snow lands on their backs, it doesn't melt. The snow sits on top of all that hair like an extra blanket, helping keep them even warmer. And in the coldest of blizzards, the oxen huddle together to share their body heat.

. . . **Arctic willows.** To see what the shrubs, wildflowers, and sedges of the tundra are like, **TURN TO PAGE 40.**

. . . **lichen and moss.** To see what the lichens and mosses of the tundra are like, **TURN TO PAGE 24.**

NORTHERN RED-BACKED VOLE

(Clethrionomys rutilus)

The northern red-backed vole gnaws at the stems of the bunchberry plants with her sharp front teeth. The gnawing not only helps her cut up her food, but it wears down her teeth too. Like all rodents' teeth, they'll grow her entire life. She has to work to keep them from growing too long and getting in her way. She breaks off a bit of stem and tucks it in her cheek. She hops over the ground and ducks into one of her underground nests. There she stashes the stem in a back tunnel—just in case she needs it later.

In the winter, the voles' tunnels lead them down to the tasty flattened grasses under the snow. In the summer, the voles nibble on roots from underground as well as on plants aboveground. Either way, their snacking fills an important role in the tundra. By dropping the moss and lichen and scattering it as they eat, the voles help it to grow in new places.

The vole pauses to scratch at a flea on her ear. Then she sets about lining her tunnel with fur and leaves. In a week or so, she'll have her second litter of babies. It'll be her last—she's already an old lady. Voles rarely live through two winters. Good thing her babies will grow quickly.

Last night for dinner, she gnawed at . . .

... more roots and stems. To see what the shrubs, wildflowers, and sedges of the tundra are like, TURN TO PAGE 40.

... a woolly bear caterpillar that fell off a shrub. To see what another caterpillar is up to, TURN TO PAGE 38.

... bunches of bunchberries. To see what the shrubs, wildflowers, and sedges of the tundra are like, TURN TO PAGE 40.

... an amphipod or two. To see what another amphipod is up to, TURN TO PAGE 16.

... lichen and moss scratched from the ground. To see what the lichens and mosses of the tundra are like, TURN TO PAGE 24.

PEREGRINE FALCON (Falco Peregrinus)

The peregrine falcon floats on the thermal—the warm air rising high above the tundra. From up here, she can see for miles—and in detail. Her eyes can see more light and focus better than human eyes can. She also has larger eyes, so what she sees looks bigger than what you see. In fact, if you could look through her eyes, you'd be able to read a page in a book from a mile (1.6 kilometers) away.

The peregrine spots something below. She presses her tail low and spreads her tail feathers. She flaps her wings at a steep angle. This makes her hover in the air like a helicopter as she focuses on her target. In the air 1,000 feet (305 m) below her, an Arctic tern flies by. In a flash, the peregrine tucks her wings in tight and points her head at the ground. She's one of the fastest creatures on the planet. She screams to the ground like a bullet shot out of a gun. Her dive, or stoop, is so fast that it's hard to even see her. Just before she reaches the tern, her speed is almost 200 miles (322 km) per hour. That's faster than most race cars!

DDT and Migration

Even though peregrine falcons are able to live all over the world, they were once in real danger of dying out. People used a chemical called DDT to kill bugs that ate their crops. But the poisoned bugs were eaten by other birds, and those birds were eaten by falcons. The chemical got into the falcons' systems and made their eggshells extra thin. When the parents sat on the eggs, the shells broke, and no new falcons could be born. Eventually, DDT was banned in places like the United States. But it's still used in some parts of the world. And since some peregrines migrate to those places, they still feed on other animals that may have DDT in their systems.

The tern never knew what hit him. The peregrine's extra-long talons snatch him midflight as she stops her free fall and flaps back up with her wings. Sometimes just the force of getting hit by something going that fast kills her **prey**. But just in case, the peregrine brings the tern up to her hooked beak and crunches through its neck bones. She's got a special notch in her beak just for breaking necks quickly.

She takes this tern back to her nest, where two chicks squawk hungrily. Perched on the rock, she hunches over, shielding her catch under the cover of her wings. She's mantling—trying to look bigger so that other birds won't steal her meal. She pins the dead bird down with her claws and rips its feathers out with her beak. The fluffy pile of feathers below her nest shows what a successful hunter she's been this summer. *Last night for dinner, the peregrine falcon brought home...*

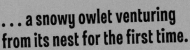

. . . **a young herring gull snatched from the sky.** To see what another gull is up to, TURN TO PAGE 58.

. . . **a young tundra swan paddling out to deeper water.** To see what another swan is up to, TURN TO PAGE 18.

. . . **a couple of collared lemmings burrowing in the ground.** To see what another lemming is up to, TURN TO PAGE 43.

. . . **an Arctic hare too far from a good hiding place.** To see what another hare is up to, TURN TO PAGE 46.

. . . **a long-tailed jaeger returning from its winter migration.** To see what another jaeger is up to, TURN TO PAGE 26.

. . . **a snowy owlet venturing from its nest for the first time.** To see what another snowy owl is up to, TURN TO PAGE 12.

. . . **an Arctic fox cub exploring the marsh.** To see what another fox is up to, TURN TO PAGE 10.

. . . **an Eskimo curlew flying in from the south.** To see what another Eskimo curlew is up to, TURN TO PAGE 15.

HORSEFLIES, MOSQUITOES, AND GNATS

It's hard to imagine the cold of the tundra as a place where insects live. But the truth is that in the summer, the Arctic tundra is alive with bugs. Clouds of them hover over the wet land, living just for a summer. Many of these insects drink nectar from the blooming plants in the tundra, but others drink the blood of animals.

A horsefly silently lands upon a caribou's leg. The caribou has just shed most of his winter fur so the fly's meal is a little easier to get to today. Before the caribou can shoo her off, the fly has sunk her knifelike mouthparts into his skin. She drinks down his blood until she's full, leaving just a drop on the skin. This little bit will attract even more insects to the poor caribou.

Only the female mosquitoes, gnats, and horseflies swarm the animals of the tundra. The males eat nectar from wildflowers. But the females need blood before they can lay eggs. After getting some blood, the horsefly will find a moist spot on the ground where her eggs can grow into **larvae** and then hatch into flies.

Last night for dinner, she drank more blood from . . .

56

Top: A horsefly
Bottom: Mosquitoes buzz over the tundra.

. . . a grizzly bear on the prowl for a meal. To see what another grizzly bear is up to, TURN TO PAGE 8.

. . . an Arctic wolf as it rests near its pack. To see what another wolf is up to, TURN TO PAGE 30.

. . . an Arctic fox trotting home to feed her young. To see what another fox is up to, TURN TO PAGE 10.

. . . a polar bear searching for a meal. To see what another polar bear is up to, TURN TO PAGE 33.

. . . a musk ox snorting and stomping to shoo the pesky flies. To see what another musk ox is up to, TURN TO PAGE 48.

. . . a wolverine snarling at a rival. To see what another wolverine is up to, TURN TO PAGE 37.

. . . an Arctic hare midhop. To see what another hare is up to, TURN TO PAGE 46.

HERRING GULL *(Larus argentatus)*

Gaw-gaw-gaw-gaw-squeee-squee! The gull isn't at all quiet about what she's doing. She dives and yanks at the chunk of caribou **carrion** in the other gull's mouth. The other gull isn't so willing to give it up, though. A midair tug-of-war begins, ending with the second gull flapping away with the hunk of meat. But the first gull lunges at her again, and this time, she finally wins the prize. She gulps it down before it can be stolen back.

With a full stomach, the winning gull heads back to her nest, a scratched-out place in the dirt where her mate and three chicks are waiting. Almost as soon as she lands, the chicks start pecking at the red dot on her bill. They're letting her know they're ready to eat. She throws up the caribou, and her babies gobble the tidbits down.

Winter Vacation

Herring gulls probably look familiar to you. These are the same gulls that you often see squawking at the beach or clustering in parking lots. Over the winter, the gulls migrate south. Many people think of them as pesky birds. That's because they swoop, screech, pester, steal food, and argue with one another in cities, just like they do on the tundra.

After the chicks are fed, her mate flies off for a snack, and the gull begins preening. Near the base of her tail is a special oil gland. She pushes it with her beak and then smoothes the oil onto her feathers. The oil keeps her feathers from getting wet. With waterproof feathers and webbed feet, she's as comfortable in the water as on land. That gives her plenty of places to look for food, and she'll eat just about anything she finds.

Last night for dinner, she brought home...

. . . a long-tailed jaeger that landed too close to the nest. To see what another jaeger is up to, TURN TO PAGE 26.

. . . a woolly bear caterpillar inching along an Arctic poppy. To see what another caterpillar is up to, TURN TO PAGE 38.

. . . sandhill crane eggs left alone too long. To see what another crane is up to, TURN TO PAGE 34.

. . . Arctic springtails springing up in front of her. To see what another springtail is up to, TURN TO PAGE 28.

. . . an Arctic wolf cub who had starved to death. To see what another wolf is up to, TURN TO PAGE 30.

. . . amphipods nibbling on dead leaves. To see what another amphipod is up to, TURN TO PAGE 16.

. . . bits of a dead Arctic fox. To see what another fox is up to, TURN TO PAGE 10.

GLOSSARY

bacteria: tiny living things made up of only one cell

carnivore: an animal that eats other animals

carrion: the decaying remains of a dead animal, which can be food for other animals

decomposers: living things, such as insects or bacteria, that feed on dead plants and animals

endangered: an animal that is in danger of dying out

extinct: no longer existing

food chain: a system in which energy moves from the sun to plants and animals as each eats and is eaten

food web: many food chains linked together

habitat: an area where a plant or animal naturally lives and grows

heliotropic: a plant that turns toward the sun to get as much sunlight as possible

larvae: insects in their wormlike stage, which occurs between the egg and adult form

mammals: animals that have hair and feed their babies milk from their bodies

migrate: to move from one area to another, usually in search of food

molt: to shed skin or feathers

nutrients: substances, especially in food, that help a plant or animal survive

perennial: occurring every year

permafrost: permanently frozen ground usually underneath soil or rock. It's found only in very cold climates.

predators: animals that hunt and kill other animals for food

prey: animals that are hunted for food by other animals

primary consumers: animals that eat plants

producers: living things, such as plants, that make their own food

secondary consumers: animals and insects that eat other animals and insects

tertiary consumers: animals that eat other animals and that have few natural enemies

tussocks: small rounded clumps of grass

FURTHER READING AND WEBSITES

Arthopolis
http://www.athropolis.com/index.htm
This site offers a great list of links to all things Arctic and tundra.

Canadian Museum of Nature
http://nature.ca/ukaliq/index_e.cfm
At this site, you can read facts and legends about the Arctic hare and discover how it fits into its tundra habitat.

Enchanted Learning
http://www.enchantedlearning.com
Type "tundra" in the search box at this site, and you'll find animal diagrams, facts, and quizzes about tundra animals.

Fleisher, Paul. *Tundra Food Webs*. Minneapolis: Lerner Publications Company, 2008. This book provides a look at the food web within the Arctic tundra.

Johansson, Philip. *The Frozen Tundra: A Web of Life*. Berkeley Heights, NJ: Enslow, 2004. Read more about the climate, seasons, plants, and animals of the tundra.

Johnson, Rebecca L. *A Walk in the Tundra*. Minneapolis: Lerner Publications Company, 2001. Go on a journey through the Arctic in this book, meeting the animals and plants of the tundra, both alpine and Arctic.

Missouri Botanical Garden
http://www.mbgnet.net/sets/tundra/index.htm
Learn about the plants, animals, climate, and people of the Arctic tundra.

SELECTED BIBLIOGRAPHY

ADF&G. "Wildlife Notebook Series." *Alaska Department of Fish and Game*. 2007. http://www.adfg.state.ak.us/pubs/notebook/notehome.php (September 10, 2008).

All Things Arctic. "Environmental Issues of the Arctic Region." *All Things Arctic*. 1998. http://www.allthingsarctic.com/environment/index.aspx (September 10, 2008).

Burnie, David. *Animal: The Definitive Visual Guide to the World's Wildlife*. Edited by Don E. Wilson. New York: DK, 2005.

Clark, Penny. *Life in the Tundra*. New York: Children's Press, 2005.

International Union for Conservation of Nature and Natural Resources. *The 2006 IUCN Red List of Endangered Species*. IUCN. N.d. http://www.iucnredlist.org (September 10, 2008).

Nearctic. "Biomes, Ecoregions, and Habitats—Tundra." *Neararctica.com*. 1999. http://www.nearctica.com/ecology/habitats/tundra.htm (September 10, 2008).

Smithsonian Institution. "Arctic Studies Center." *Smithsonian National Museum of Natural History*. 2002. http://www.mnh.si.edu/arctic/index.html (September 10, 2008).

University of Michigan Museum of Zoology. *Animal Diversity Web*. 2008. http://animaldiversity.ummz.umich.edu (September 10, 2008).

U.S. Fish and Wildlife Service. "Arctic National Wildlife Refuge." *U.S. Fish and Wildlife Service—Alaska*. N.d. http://arctic.fws.gov (September 10, 2008).

Woodford, Chris. *Arctic Tundra and Polar Deserts*. Austin, TX: Raintree Steck-Vaughn, 2002.

INDEX

Photo Acknowledgments

The images in this book are used with the permission of: © Steve McCutcheon/ Visuals Unlimited, pp. 1, 4-5, 6-7, 9, 11, 14, 17,19, 22, 25, 27, 29, 32, 36, 39, 42, 45, 47, 49, 51, 55, 57, 59; © Bill Hauser/Independent Picture Service, pp. 5, 40 (right); © Dave Welling/drr.net, p. 8; © Norbert Rosing/Photolibrary/ Getty Images, p. 10; © Steven Kazlowski/Science Faction/Getty Images, p. 12; © Kim Taylor/Minden Pictures, p.13 (top); © Michio Hoshino/Minden Pictures, p. 13 (bottom); Curlew illustration reproduced with permission from the Canadian Museum of Nature, Ottawa, Canada, p. 15; Courtesy of Rolf Gradinger/ NOAA, p. 16; © Wayne Lynch/All Canada Photos/Alamy, pp. 18, 43; © Paul Souders/Danita Delimont/drr.net, p. 20; © Tom and Pat Leeson, pp. 21, 53; © Fred Hirschmann/Science Faction/Getty Images, p. 24 (inset); © Tim Hauf/ Visuals Unlimited, p. 24 (bottom); © Roberto Lerco, pp. 26, 58; © Michael Worland/BAS, NERC, p. 28; © Jim Brandenburg/Minden Pictures, p. 30; © iStockphoto.com/Paul Loewen, p. 31; © Thomas Mangelsen/Minden Pictures, p. 33; © Steve Kazlowski/Danita Delimont/drr.net, pp. 34, 37; © Ron Sanford/ CORBIS, p. 35; © Charles Mann/Photo Researchers, Inc., p. 38 (top); courtesy of B. M. Drees, Department of Entomology, Texas A&M University, p. 38 (bottom); © 2008 Patrick Endres/Alaska Stock, p. 40 (left); © Stephen J. Krasemann/Photo Researchers, Inc. p. 41 (top); © Eastcott Momatuik/Digital Vision/Getty Images, p. 41 (bottom); © Mark Chappel/Animals Animals, p. 44; © Paul Nicklen/National Geographic/Getty Images, pp. 46 (left), 48; © Art Wolfe/The Image Bank/Getty Images, p. 46 (right); © Michael S. Quinton/ National Geographic/Getty Images, p. 50; © John Waters/naturepl.com, p. 52 (top); © Pete Cairns/naturepl.com, p. 52 (bottom); © Jorma Luhta/naturepl .com, p. 54 (top); © Dietmar Nill/naturepl.com, p. 54 (bottom); © Michael Durham/Minden Pictures/Getty Images, p. 56 (top); © Michael Giannechini/ Photo Researchers, Inc., p. 56 (bottom); Illustrations for game board and pieces © Bill Hauser/Independent Picture Service.

Front cover (main): © Steve McCutcheon/Visuals Unlimited; (thumbnails): © Steve Kazlowski/Danita Delimont//drr.net (far left), © Stephen J. Krasemann/ DRK PHOTO (second from left); U.S. Fish and Wildlife Service (second from right and far right).

About the Authors

Don Wojahn and Becky Wojahn are school library media specialists by day and writers by night. Their natural habitat is the temperate forests of northwestern Wisconsin, where they share their den with two animal-loving sons and two big black dogs. The Wojahns' other Follow that Food Chain books include *A Desert Food Chain, A Rain Forest Food Chain, A Savanna Food Chain, A Temperate Forest Food Chain,* and *An Australian Outback Food Chain.*